OPTIMIZING THE TAX CODE

Practical Tips and Legal Strategies to Earn and Keep More of Your Hard-Earned Money into Retirement

HOLLIS DAY JR.

ISBN: 978-1-950043-24-8

Publishing services provided by:

Archangel Ink
Publishing Services. By Authors, For Authors

To the taxpayers of America—the people who get
up and go to work every day, who do their job
without exception to provide for their families.

Contents

Introduction

I'm an entrepreneur at heart. I think that's why my interest in investing grew into a business opportunity. I started learning about financial strategies in 2001 after managing nursing homes for seven years. Like so many people at that time, I lost money in my 401(k) because of the market downturn. I hadn't done anything wrong to lose that money. It wasn't like I'd blown it at a casino. I was furious when I saw how little control I had over the outcome after working so hard to invest in my 401(k). I wanted to see what other options were out there so I could decide what to do with my own money.

By 2008 I'd learned a lot and had found my niche. I was hooked. I read tons of books and articles on investing. I hunted down experts in the field. I learned all I could from Mike Tolleson, original franchisee of Cicis Pizza, taking notes and signing up for training sessions. I loved this stuff. But it didn't really become personal until I suddenly realized my parents had gotten ripped off.

My mom and dad were hardworking blue-collar middle-class people. After working as a wife and a mom, my mother went back to school to become a nurse. She worked long hours and overnight shifts for as long as I can remember. My dad and my uncle owned a tire business together called Day Brothers Tire across the river from Baton Rouge in Port Allen. Anybody within a hundred-mile radius that wanted a bumper, a winch, big four-wheel-drive tires, or a lift kit had to come to Dad's shop—his was the only place around in the late sixties that offered those items. I spent a lot of hours after school helping my dad in the tire shop. Hard times hit in the early nineties, and my dad had to shut down the shop and go to work for a tire distributor run by a family friend.

A decade later, in June 2006, my mom passed away after a battle with ovarian cancer, and my dad died unexpectedly seventeen months later on Thanksgiving Day of 2007. My mother was fifty-four at the time of her death; my father sixty-four at his. My parents had paid into Social Security and Medicare every year of their working lives, expecting to get their checks when the time came.

But it didn't work out that way. My mother was four months shy of qualifying for disability when she died. All that overtime my mother worked, all those 12- to 16-hour shifts, all those nights she logged as a nurse … she never received a penny from Social Security and Medicare. My dad received a $255 check from the government to help pay for burial expenses. That's it. That didn't even pay for the flowers!

Where did all her money go? The funds the government took from my mom all those years … where was it? It sure wasn't sent to my dad. It wasn't passed on to my sister and me. It was gone.

In October of 2007, my dad decided to start drawing his Social Security when he turned sixty-five, in March of the next year. So I took my dad to the Social Security office in Baton Rouge. He handed over his ID, verified his Social Security number, and said, "I'd like to start drawing my Social Security on my sixty-fifth birthday." They agreed he would start receiving payments in March of 2008 and told him, to the penny, how much his payments were going to be.

Cool deal, right? Well, he died the next month of a pulmonary embolism. Just like my mom, my dad never saw a single penny of that money after all those years the government forced him to pay in.

My parents would have been better off hiding money under their mattress their whole lives than entrusting it to the federal government.

Four years later, as I reflected on this experience, it was like a fire was lit under me. I didn't want anyone else to have the rug pulled out from under them like my parents had. The entrepreneur in me was trying to figure out how to solve this problem.

I found my answer in Sunnyvale, Texas, after attending a training by Mike Tolleson. During dinner at Mike's house, I met Mark McKay, co-host of *Smart Money Radio* in Amarillo, Texas. I listened with rapt attention as he described his show, which focuses on tax management, alternative investment strategies, and helping the average person navigate retirement.

I decided not to stay in my hotel that night. I was too pumped up. I grabbed my stuff, checked out, and got back on the road. As the miles passed, I couldn't stop thinking about Mark's story. I just thought, *Why can't I do that in Baton Rouge?* About the time I reached Ruston, it was two in the morning and I couldn't keep my eyes open anymore. I'd spent a lot of time in this town when I went to school here, so it felt like a safe place to stop for a rest. I pulled off the road into the Louisiana Tech baseball parking lot, leaned my seat back, and promptly fell asleep. Sometime later, I woke to a fierce knocking on my window and a glaring light in my face. I rolled down the window to hear a police officer asking for my license and registration. I just pointed to the alumni sticker on my car, but he wasn't satisfied. He didn't care who I was, I wasn't allowed to sleep there.

I grabbed a coffee and got back on the road. That idea of hosting a radio show was still there waiting for me. And it only grew with every passing minute. I was so obsessed about hosting a show about alternative investment strategies that I didn't go home—I drove straight to WJBO in Baton Rouge and knocked on the door at 6:00 a.m. I set up a meeting with the station director and pitched the idea for an alternative investment show. A couple months later, I got the green light.

Unfortunately, my parents' story isn't unique. People call in to my radio show all the time to share stories eerily similar to theirs. The details may be a little different, but the message is always the same: they got blindsided by government regulations and taxes that robbed them and their families of their hard-earned inheritance.

I'm not here to help you scam the system. The work I do with clients and on my radio show is about education. I want to help people understand the laws and the internal revenue code and become empowered within the system so they can make the most of their financial choices.

That's what this book is about. I'll demystify the tax code, give you tax-friendly money-making strategies, and teach you legal ways of doing what's best for your money. If you believe you know best how to take care of your hard-earned money, you've come to the right place. I can give you the knowledge and tools to do just that.

Chapter 1

History of the Tax Code and Prediction of Future Tax Rates

America is a land of taxation that
was founded to avoid taxation.
—Laurence J. Peter

I see a lot of people setting themselves up for trouble in retirement. These are smart, hardworking people just like you doing what they've been told to do. They log their time at work, faithfully contribute to their 401(k), and trust that when they need it, their investment is going to come through for them.

Experts who encourage you to bank on your 401(k) are peddling the message:

Don't pay now—pay later!

Sound familiar? It sounds good. It might even feel good. It's comforting to just let your automatic draft stock away your money every month without effort on your part. There's a kind of peace of mind with this strategy—*I'm saving for retirement!*

The problem is, it rarely turns out that way.

What We Can Learn from the History of the Tax Code

A quick look at the history of the tax code paints an unsettling picture.

Taxes, in various forms, are as old as our nation itself. In the early days, our fledgling government used tariffs on imports to raise needed funds. Wartime often required new taxes to be levied, which expired when the war was over. The Stamp Act was passed in 1797, taxing wills, personal estates, and possessions of the deceased, but was repealed five years later. Apart from a few hiccups, this method of short-term increase in taxation worked for a while. Then came the Revolutionary War, and with it a pile of national debt. To counteract this, an excise tax was imposed on distilled beverages and eventually repealed.

The government managed to keep debt under control during peace time, but with every war we fought, the debt spiked. Once again, a tax would be imposed to restore the balance. The first tax on income appeared in 1861 when funds were needed to finance the Civil War.[1] Rates rose in 1862 and again in 1864, and the tax was repealed in 1872.

Debates raged about whether this practice of taxing personal income was unconstitutional, leading to ratifying the 16th Amendment in 1913, allowing Congress to tax all types of income. By 1918, income tax was helping to finance World War I.

Income tax was here to stay. Over the years, the number of income brackets and tax rates has fluctuated wildly. Exemptions and deductions were added to make it seem like less of a burden on taxpayers. And yet federal reliance on the income tax grew with each year: "In 1916, income taxes had been providing 16% of federal revenue. From 1917 to 1920, that percentage ranged as high as 58%. The tax was now a pillar of federal finance."[2]

Add to our tax burden the reality of our ever more bloated national debt. Regardless of who is in the White House, our debt load increases year after year. That number is not going anywhere, and no amount of progressive tax reform is going to solve it.

---

1 "A History of Taxes in America," accuratetax.com, May 16, 2017, www.accuratetax.com/blog/history-taxes-america/.

2 "Tax History Museum: 1901–1932, The Income Tax Arrives," Tax Analysts, accessed September 16, 2020, www.taxhistory.org/www/website.nsf/Web/THM1901.

What You Should Do about It

Financial advisors will try to soften the blow by telling you that retirement will put you into a lower tax bracket. Don't worry about that mounting debt—just keep tucking that money into your 401(k) every month, and you can draw what you need in retirement at that lower rate. The truth is more complicated than that. There are many factors that determine what tax bracket you'll be in, and an advisor shouldn't be forecasting that about your future. Do yourself a favor, if an advisor tells you this: RUN.

While that may be true for certain rare individuals, the vast majority of hardworking people cannot stake their future on that claim. Even if you are in the same tax bracket when you retire, you likely won't have the write-offs you have now. Think about it—the kids will be grown, the mortgage could be paid off, and student loans will be a distant memory.

Pay later isn't looking so good now, is it? Add to that the fact that today's tax brackets are at an all-time low. With rising national debt and historically low tax brackets, there has never been a better time to use after-tax dollars for investing. Tax rates *will be higher* in the future. I just don't see a way around that. Stop kicking your tax can down the road.

But you like your 401(k), you say? You're not ready to

give it up? What if I told you the 401(k) wasn't designed for the masses? It was never meant to house the wealth of the working public. Would that change your mind?

Chapter 2

Story of the 401(k)

The government's view of the economy could be summed up in a few short phrases: If it moves, tax it. If it keeps moving, regulate it. And if it stops moving, subsidize it.
—Ronald Reagan

The taxpayer—that's someone who works for the federal government but doesn't have to take the civil service examination.
—Ronald Reagan

Have you ever wondered how the 401(k) started? If you're banking on your 401(k) for retirement bliss, you might be in for a rude awakening. The 401(k) wasn't originally designed for the way it's being used today. Plus, it's evolved over the last three decades to be an even more complicated system. Let's take a look at how the 401(k) was created and some complaints about the current system. Then you be the judge of whether this is still the right strategy for your investment.

History of the 401(k)

The 401(k) was created in 1980 by Ted Benna, a retirement benefit consultant for the Johnson Companies. Benna wasn't looking to revolutionize retirement savings. He was trying to solve a problem for a bank client when he realized Section 401(k) of the IRS Code allowed for the very thing the client was requesting. What was that exactly? Benna explains:

> The bank wanted to replace its cash bonus plan with a tax-deferred profit sharing plan where employees wouldn't have access to the money until they left the bank. The president wanted to add this type of plan because the president wanted the tax break and the bank needed the plan to be competitive with other area banks.[3]

This was a great deal for the bank's president and other high-paid employees looking for a tax break. But what about

---

3 "A Brief History of 401K," Benna 401K, accessed September 16, 2020, http://benna401k.com/401k-history.html.

employees who weren't pulling in big bonuses? How did this benefit them? It wasn't until Benna added employer matching that the plan become attractive to lower-paid employees too.

Problems with the Modern 401(k)

While Benna's brainchild spawned a savings plan revolution, the 401(k) system has evolved beyond its original purpose and the spirit in which it was created. Today's 401(k) plans are not passing muster under increased scrutiny. Here are five common complaints you should take a hard look at:[4,5]

- **Tax-deferral is uncertain.** It might sound like a good deal to defer paying taxes on retirement savings, but as we discussed in chapter 1, it's highly unlikely tax rates will be better in the future. If they go up, you'll be paying higher taxes on all that money you worked so diligently to save. That's a big risk. Are you really willing to take it with so little evidence it will be worth it?

---

4 John Sullivan, "6 Reasons the 401k is a 'Scam' (Wait, What?)," 401(k) Specialist, July 12, 2017, https://401kspecialistmag.com/6-reasons-401k-scam-wait/.

5 Peter Reagan, "6 Reasons Why 401(k) Plans Are a Rip-Off," Townhall, March 5, 2019, https://townhall.com/columnists/peterreagan/2019/03/05/6-reasons-why-401k-plans-are-a-ripoff-n2542394.

- **You give up control.** Contributing to your 401(k) means you can't touch that money until you're 59.5 years old. Try and access it before then and you'll be penalized for seeking control of your money. Then when you turn 70.5, you'll be forced to start withdrawing funds, which will trigger the tax payments on those funds.

- **Employer matching isn't what you think it is.** This seems like free money on the surface, but employer matching isn't everything it's cracked up to be. It can take up to six years for your employer match funds to be fully vested, so if you leave the company before that time, you may be losing some of those funds you were counting on.

- **Plan fees set you back.** Do you take the time to read the disclosure on your 401(k) plan fees? If you're like most people, you don't. That means you don't know how much of your contribution is actually going to your account. If you do know the percentage you're paying and it seems like a small sacrifice, try multiplying it by the decades you're paying it until retirement. It's not such a small amount when you look at it that way.

- **You're at the mercy of the market's whim.** Anyone watching their 401(k) during the 2008 recession knows what a punch in the gut it is to see your hard-earned retirement savings plummet. When the market is good, you might be feeling great! But the reality is the volatility of the market is one more factor keeping you from having control of your retirement savings.

It's not just disgruntled bloggers badmouthing the 401(k) strategy. Even Benna admits that the modern 401(k) has grown out of control. "He'd created 'a monster' that should be 'blown up,'" Benna lamented in 2011.[6]

Here's what it comes down to: You're in a government-sponsored program, and Uncle Sam is your partner. If you have any money in a 401(k)—IRA, SEP, any of those—the government, the career politicians in Washington who are pulling the strings, will be dictating to you what you'll pay when you're ready to withdraw your money. Is that how you want to treat your hard-earned wages?

---

6 Jeremy Olshan, "The inventor of the 401(k) says he created a 'monster,'" MarketWatch, September 26, 2016, www.marketwatch.com/story/the-inventor-of-the-401k-says-he-created-a-monster-2016-05-16.

Now What?

I'm fed up with the traditional retirement savings route. What about you? Are you ready to consider some alternatives? In the following pages, you'll read about different strategies for investing your money that will give you more control over your investments, greater certainty about future returns, and deeper peace of mind for retirement.

Chapter 3

Investing in Oil and Gas without Giving an Arm and a Leg

There is no such thing as a good tax.

—Winston Churchill

We contend that for a nation to try to tax itself into prosperity is like a man standing in a bucket and trying to lift himself up by the handle.

—Winston Churchill

So, if investing in a 401(k) isn't as solid an approach as we once thought, what other options are out there? By far one of the most promising investment opportunities today is in oil and gas. Did you know the IRS has an Oil and Gas Handbook? That's because "the importance of the petroleum industry to the economy of the United States has led Congress to pass specialized tax laws that are unique to the oil and gas industry."[7]

Don't be fooled by political rhetoric: oil and gas aren't going anywhere anytime soon. I have a deep respect and sense of responsibility to this planet. Sustainable alternatives are important, but the truth is that hydrocarbons are going to be an essential part of our energy use for the foreseeable future.

According to The National Academy of Sciences:[8]

> The United States gets 81% of its total energy from oil, coal, and natural gas, all of which are fossil fuels. We depend on those fuels to heat our homes, run our vehicles, power industry and manufacturing, and provide us with electricity. Eventually, the degree to which we depend on fossil fuels will have to decline … In the meantime, how do we use fossil fuels in the most efficient and environmentally responsible way possible?

Since Reagan's presidency, our government has sought to decrease our dependence on foreign oil. One way they do this

---

7 IRM §4.41.1.1.2(4)

8 "Fossil Fuels," The National Academies, accessed September 18, 2020, http://needtoknow.nas.edu/energy/energy-sources/fossil-fuels/.

is to offer tax benefits to investors in the domestic oil and gas industry. The risks to investors have greatly decreased in the years since, and technology has advanced by leaps and bounds. The benefits offered by the government have been available for decades, and they're only getting better. For example, the Tax Cuts and Jobs Act of 2017 reduced the corporate tax rate from 35% to 21%, of particular interest to oil and gas companies.

Resolute Capital Partners (RCP), a company with expert knowledge and experience in the field, identifies five major benefits of investing in oil and gas:[9]

1. Intangible Drilling Costs
2. Active versus Passive Income
3. Alternative Minimum Tax Liability
4. Depreciation of Equipment Costs
5. The Depletion Allowance

---

9 "Energy Boost: Understanding the Potential Tax Benefits of U.S. Oil & Gas Investments," Resolute Capital Partners, accessed September 16, 2020. This whitepaper is only available with login credentials. To access this whitepaper directly, visit www.resolutecapitalpartners.com/investor and submit an Investor/Partner Inquiry to obtain login credentials.

Intangible Drilling Costs

Imagine funding an oil well up front. Think of all the supplies, manpower, fuel, and gear required for such a massive project. These are referred to as intangible drilling costs (IDCs), and they are incurred before a drop of oil is collected. You can see the risks involved for companies and their investors. The government rewards this risk to investors by allowing them to write off 100% of all IDCs.

RCP[10] puts this in perspective:

> Say you invest in an oil property in June 2019, but exploration is slow, and drilling is not due to start until December 2019. The tax code says you still have a 3-month cushion to start drilling—so by the end of March 2020—while still claiming the benefits in the year they were incurred.

Active versus Passive Income

Active income is income earned in return for services; this includes "wages, tips, salaries, commissions and income

---

10 "Energy Boost," accessed September 16, 2020.

from businesses in which there is material participation."[11] Passive income is regular income you earn without putting in consistent effort. But did you know that they're treated differently by the IRS in terms of taxation?

In the eyes of the IRS, passive income includes "net rental income" or "income from a business in which the taxpayer does not materially participate."

RCP explains the implications for investors in oil and gas:

> Unlike a royalty interest, a working interest in an oil and gas property is not considered a passive activity under the current tax code. As such, all net losses from oil and gas investments may be offset against other forms of income, such as wages and capital gains.

What this means for you as the investor is that by investing in an oil and gas property *you could potentially write off the full amount of the investment that you make.*

---

11 Ali Boone, "The Truth about Active Income vs. Passive Income," BiggerPockets, accessed September 18, 2020, https://www.biggerpockets.com/blog/2013-11-09-active-income-vs-passive-income.

Alternative Minimum Viable Tax Liability

We all love tax deductions, but there's only so much you can deduct before you're no longer shouldering your fair share of the tax burden. To ensure taxpayers are paying what they should, the government enforces the Alternative Minimum Tax (AMT), which limits how much someone can deduct in a year. "When the AMT is triggered, an investor no longer gets the full benefit of all possible deductions."[12]

Oil and gas companies are sensitive to this aspect of the tax code for their investors and commonly take steps to compensate by maximizing the IDC deductions. The RCP whitepaper explains:

> Specifically, an oil and gas company may incur costs in 2018, but hold off paying the invoice until 2019 so as to extend the deduction benefit over two years—and hence maximize deductions in years 2018 and 2019, without triggering the AMT.... According to the IRS, an investor may deduct IDC costs as a current business expense by subtracting it from your income in either the year you incur it or the year you pay it.

---

12 "Energy Boost," accessed September 16, 2020.

As you can see, the oil and gas companies go the extra mile to benefit investors, yet another reason why this is such a great money-making strategy.

Depreciation of Equipment Costs

Another benefit to investors in oil and gas is a century-old provision allowing for 100% of tangible costs in the form of equipment maintenance to be written off. Think pumps, tanks, tubes, casing, etc. RCP explains, "Historically, an investor has been able to write off 100% of these expenses through depreciation deductions over a 7-year time period."[13]

While this benefit isn't quite as attractive as IDC deductions, it is becoming more attractive because of the new tax laws, which grant investors the extra benefit of "a depreciation deduction equal to 100% of the costs of 'qualifying property' in the year the property is placed into service." Another excellent deduction oil and gas investors can count on in the coming years.

The Depletion Allowance

Because oil and gas are limited resources, drilling is steadily depleting the reserves. RCP explains, "Because you are

13 "Energy Boost," accessed September 16, 2020.

forever reducing the oil you have access to, the tax code grants certain oil and gas producers a depletion allowance of 15% on the gross income earned on the average daily production of up to 1,000 barrels of oil, or 6 million cubic feet of gas (Internal Revenue Code Sec. 613A(c))."

In the past, these costs were depreciated over a seven-year period. But thanks to the changes made in the Tax Cuts and Jobs Act of 2017, you can now count on those costs being 100% tax deductible in the first year of investment.

Did you notice that term "certain oil and gas producers"? This allowance doesn't apply to large producers, meaning those refining over 50,000 barrels a day, those averaging in excess of 75,000 barrels in daily refinery runs, and retail producers. RCP puts this in perspective:

> So for instance, if an oil producer generates 800 barrels of oil each day at $100 a barrel, it will not be taxed at $100 a barrel, but rather $85. Large companies with extensive holdings, like ExxonMobil, do not receive this benefit.

You can see the potential this creates for investors to partner with small private companies in the industry in need of capital up front to fund their drilling projects.

Getting Started

Investing in oil and gas is one of the best financial strategies for decreasing your tax burden, and the benefits are only getting better. The government is so committed to this industry that they put very few limitations on income or net worth. What other industry can boast such attractive tax breaks?

Unfortunately, this is a strategy you can't access through a traditional broker. Brokerage firms don't have access to private oil and gas companies. Most of these deals are private equity deals. When my clients hear about this opportunity, they're surprised at how simple it is. Many start investing in oil and gas immediately. Fortunately, I specialize in connecting clients with this type of alternative investment. So, if this sounds like the right opportunity for you, I'd love to help you get started investing with oil and gas. Visit sagemoneyradio.com and click Contact to send me an email.

Chapter 4

Cost Segregation for Commercial Building Owners

We have a system that increasingly taxes work and subsidizes nonwork.

—Milton Friedman

Another great option for decreasing your taxable income is called *cost segregation*. This is an option available to commercial property owners and tenants. Think of properties like warehouses, offices, retail malls, hotels and motels, shopping strips, self-storage facilities, dealerships, restaurants and franchises, apartments and condos, medical and dental facilities, assisted living centers, supermarkets, and banks. If that's you, take note of this great strategy.

First off, what is cost segregation? Cost segregation is a method approved by the IRS allowing commercial property owners to accelerate depreciation and reduce their tax burden. This generates substantial savings, creating cash flow for owners to reinvest in their business, apply to their principal payments, or spend however they see fit.

For business owners, this is an amazing tool to invest funds back into the business without having to partner with a third party. Let's dig a little deeper and look at how it works. With cost segregation, you can:

- **Cut taxable income.** By accelerating depreciation, you owe less in federal taxes.
- **Bump up cash flow.** Paying less in taxes means increased cash flow! This works by changing components and improvements of your commercial building from real property to personal property. The assets can then be depreciated on a much lower schedule than usual. In this way, your taxable income is significantly reduced and cash flow is dramatically increased.
- **Expand your business.** More cash flow means you can reinvest in your business or expand your current operations.

As a real-world example, consider the following case study:

> Without a Cost Segregation study, a $2.6 million apartment building in Jenks, OK, purchased in 2019 would have generated a first year depreciation of $38,888.89. By applying a cost segregation study, the property investors accelerate depreciation for the first year to $1,160,787.96. This acceleration in deprecation allows the property investors to reduce their tax liability and in turn increase their bottom line. By breaking down the building asset into components, a cost segregation also aids in future benefits of abandonment, repairs, routine maintenance and overall asset management.[14]

If you own a commercial property, don't pass up this opportunity! Get in touch, and let's talk about how you can make cost segregation work for you.

---

14 "Cost Segregation study on a $2.6 Million Apartment Building in Jenks, OK," Engineered Tax Services, accessed October 16, 2020, https://engineeredtaxservices.com/wp-content/uploads/2020/01/Cost-Segregation-Study-Apartment-Building-Jenks-OK-2019.pdf.

Tax Strategies for Business Owners

Thanks to the Tax Cuts and Jobs Act and the 2014 Tangible Property Regulations (TPRs), "Building owners … have the ability to capture $30,000 to $80,000 in income-tax savings in the first year of ownership."[15] Savvy businesspeople will ask what they can do to make the most of this reform and lower their tax burden.

Warren Dazzio, Executive Vice President of CSSI, recommends the following five strategies:[16]

1. **Apply safe harbors.** TPRs determine what business owners are required to capitalize or allowed to expense. This is where safe harbors come in. Safe harbors let you expense some expenditures rather than capitalize them.
    a. The De Minimis Safe Harbor allows an owner to expense an item of $2,500 or less.
    b. The Routine Maintenance Safe Harbor is another attractive option that allows the owner

---

15 Warren Dazzio, "Tax Reform Strategies and Self-Storage: Strategies to Improve Facility Cash Flow," Inside Self-Storage, November 18, 2019, www.insideselfstorage.com/tax-issues/tax-reform-and-self-storage-strategies-improve-facility-cash-flow.

16 Warren Dazzio, Cost Segregation Services Incorporated, https://www.costsegregationservices.com.

to expense an expenditure to a building that will need to be replaced within a ten-year timeframe.

c. The Small Taxpayer Safe Harbor offers benefits to owners who have a facility with multiple buildings.

2. **Use the ratio test to expense repairs.** When it comes to expenditures, there is very specific tax code guidance about what should be capitalized as an "improvement" or expensed as a "repair." Something called the ratio test will be used to maximize what you can expense. You can do this during the year as well as during a year-end audit.

3. **Reduce income taxes by accelerating depreciation.** After maximizing your expenses, you'll want to look at how depreciation will save or defer taxes. According to the tax code, business owners can depreciate their property by *straight-line depreciation* or by a *cost segregation study*. Using straight-line depreciation, owners can offset income every year for 39 years by 1/39th of the cost of their buildings. As I mentioned

above, an engineering-based cost segregation study breaks a building into various parts and accelerates the depreciation of parts into shorter tax lives. In this way, the larger amount of the depreciation offsets revenue and lowers income tax.

4. **Make the most of tax reform.** Through a cost segregation study, you can tap into some of the benefits afforded by the Tax Cuts and Jobs Act. New construction and additions qualify for Section 179 and 100% bonus depreciation, which means accessing deductions immediately rather than spreading the depreciation out over many years.

5. **Use a partial asset disposition to expense items you're throwing away.** Instead of capitalizing a renovation or remodel, expense portions that qualify under a partial asset disposition. A partial asset disposition allows owners to declare the remaining value of items removed during a renovation. This benefit only exists in the same tax year as the renovation occurred.

A cost segregation study will give you access to the benefits and strategies discussed above. The study takes place over a period of four to six weeks and requires the owner or tenant to provide a current tax depreciation schedule, building cost information, and change orders.[17] The process requires the commercial building components to be identified and analyzed so that the study can decide which components are eligible for accelerated depreciation.

If you own a commercial building built after December 31, 1986, you may be able to take advantage of this approach to decreasing your taxable income. This strategy could save you on taxes and put money back into your business. Check today to see if you qualify!

---

17 "Answers to Your Questions about Cost Segregation Compliance," Cost Segregation Services Incorporated, accessed September 22, 2020, www.costsegregationservices.com/cost-segregation-compliance-questions/.

Chapter 5

Restricted Trust for Business Owners

When there's a single thief, it's robbery. When there are a thousand thieves, it's taxation.

—Vanya Cohen

What if I told you there's an investment that could *guarantee* better results than an alternative investment earning 8%?[18]

You'd give me the squinty eye and ask, "What's the catch?" Right? I know you would because that's what I did when I first learned about this strategy. But after doing my homework, I can vouch for this opportunity. If you qualify for this, you're going to love it. I'll give you an overview here so you know if you qualify. If that's you, I'd love to discuss the logistics with you in more detail.

---

18 "Restricted Property Trust: Concept Overview and Illustrations," Momentum Advanced Planning, www.slideshare.net/LeeRogers5/restricted-property-trust-61925598.

What I'm referring to is called a *restricted trust*. A *trust* is "a fiduciary relationship in which one party, known as the trustor, gives another party, the trustee, the right to hold title to property or assets for the benefit of a third party, the beneficiary … A trust can be used to determine how a person's money should be managed and distributed … [and] helps avoid taxes and probate."[19]

A *restricted* trust has very specific guidelines for how it's used.

Here's how a restricted trust works. You get medically underwritten and approved for life insurance. Then you choose a charity, a nonprofit, a church, etc. that will own the policy. You make tax-deductible contributions in five-year increments, and after the term expires, you withdraw a portion of your money tax-free. "Fully tax-deductible contributions are made by the business to [a restricted trust] for a select group of participants. Of this, a portion is considered current taxable income to the participant. The remaining contribution funds the life insurance and is not considered taxable income to the participant."[20]

---

19 Julia Kagan, "Trust," Investopedia, October 19, 2020, https://www.investopedia.com/terms/t/trust.asp.

20 "Restricted Property Trust: Concept Overview and Illustrations," Momentum Advanced Planning.

Did you catch that? Unlike with 401(k) or Roth IRA contributions, this strategy allows for BOTH tax-deductible contributions and tax deferment. What a deal!

Benefits of a restricted trust include "annual income tax savings, tax-deferred asset growth, fully deductible contributions for employers, creditor protection, flexible participation parameters, death benefit protection and greater returns on plan assets."[21]

I know—you're still waiting to hear what the catch is. There's no catch, but there are limitations that may disqualify you from taking advantage of this strategy.

You can't invest funds from an employer, meaning that your income must come from an S-corp, C-corp, partnership, or LLC. You have to meet the minimum contribution amount, which for some can be a deterrent. You must commit to funding the policy in five-year increments. And you can't access the cash in the policy until it's done funding, unlike a regular life insurance policy that allows you to borrow from the cash after three years. At the end of the policy, the trust turns ownership back to you.

---

21 "Restricted Property Trust: Concept Overview and Illustrations," Momentum Advanced Planning.

So, there you have it. This is not an opportunity suited to everyone. *But* for a self-employed high-income earner who is going to be paying into life insurance anyway, what a deal! This is a fabulous vehicle for business owners to mitigate income taxes and appreciate assets at the same time. It's unheard of to find a strategy that allows these to happen simultaneously.

I am so excited about this opportunity. No one else is talking about this and, though it is for a niche group, what an amazing opportunity to drop people down an income tax bracket or two!

If you want to tap this opportunity and get a tax deduction for your contributions to life insurance, get in touch with me today. I will get you set up!

Chapter 6

The Not-So-Secure Part of Social Security

Income taxes are responsible for the transformation of the federal government from one of limited powers into a vast leviathan whose tentacles reach into almost every aspect of American life.

—Ron Paul

One thing is clear: The Founding Fathers never intended a nation where citizens would pay nearly half of everything they earn to the government.

—Ron Paul

Remember my parents' unfortunate experiences with drawing Social Security? At a time when they needed that system to come through for them, it failed them miserably. Their story is not unique. Many hardworking Americans faithfully pay into Social Security and get little to nothing in return.

The Ghost of Social Security Past

The concept of retirement is a fairly new construct. Hundreds of years ago if you were fortunate enough to make it to old age, your kids and grandkids would care for you. Visions of grandmas snapping beans on the front porch come to mind. Today younger people pay taxes to fund benefits for older people who have retired. You can see the similarities. In the past it would be your kids working to take care of you in your retirement. Now we're doing that collectively.

The irony, of course, is that Social Security was created to guard *against* economic insecurity. The Social Security Act became law in 1935. Here's how the Social Security Administration describes the climate at that time:

> The nation was deep in the throes of the Depression. Confidence in the old institutions was shaken. Social changes that started with the Industrial Revolution had long ago passed the point of no return. The traditional sources of economic security: assets; labor; family; and charity, had all failed in one degree or another. Radical proposals for action were springing like weeds from the soil of the nation's

discontent.[22]

But in the years since that time, our economy, our culture, and our society have changed drastically. The conditions that made Social Security useful in the 1930s no longer exist. We moved past the devastation of the Depression and made strides to rebuild those systems of assets, labor, family, and charity. People are living much longer now than they did in the 1930s, which means these retirement benefits are being paid out much longer than they were originally intended to.

Another strain on the system was added beneficiaries. In its original form, this law was designed to pay retired workers age 65 or older a continuing income after retirement. Later amendments to the law included "disabled workers, spouses and young children of deceased or disabled workers, and the spouses and survivors of retirees."[23] Other changes included expected retirement age and payment amounts for retirees who delayed claiming benefits past retirement age up until

22 "Historical Background and Development of Social Security," Social Security Administration, accessed on September 24, 2020, www.ssa.gov/history/briefhistory3.html.

23 Wade Pfau, "A Brief History of Social Security," *Forbes*, October 27, 2015, www.forbes.com/sites/wadepfau/2015/10/27/brief-history-of-social-security/#54b4bde153d9.

age 70.[24]

The Ghost of Social Security Present

A series of alarming shifts in the 80s and 90s allowed Social Security benefits to become taxable. In its article "The Tax-Trap Set 36 Years Ago," Bad Uncle Sam[25] explains:

> Beginning in 1984, up to 50% of Social Security and Railroad Retirement Tier I benefits became taxable for individuals whose provisional income exceeded $25,000. The threshold is $32,000 for married couples. Provisional income equals adjusted gross income (total income from all sources recognized for tax purposes) plus certain otherwise tax-exempt income, including half of Social Security and Railroad Retirement Tier I benefits....
>
> In 1993, the Omnibus Budget Reconciliation Act increased the share of some Social Security and Railroad Retirement Tier I benefits that are taxable. That

---

24 Emily Brandon, "The History of Your Social Security Payments," March 4, 2019, https://money.usnews.com/money/retirement/social-security/articles/the-history-of-your-social-security-payments.

25 "The Tax-Trap Set 36 Years Ago," Bad Uncle Sam, November 28, 2019, https://www.badunclesam.com/.

law taxes up to 85% of benefits for individuals whose provisional income exceeds $34,000 and for married couples whose provisional income exceeds $44,000.

A lot of promises were made when a lot of factors were different. People are living longer. People who never paid into the system are now receiving benefits. That's the reason things are going south. And if we want to be real about what's happening, let's call it like it is. This is double taxation! The contributions you made to Social Security were after-tax dollars pulled from your paycheck by the federal government. Now the benefit you're drawing from the system you helped fund may be subject to a tax again.

Today it takes a certain number of workers paying into the system. They call this the worker to retiree ratio. The Social Security Administration has said that they need a minimum of 2.8 workers paying into the system for every retiree collecting benefits. This requires steady population growth.

The Ghost of Social Security Yet to Come

If this ratio gets too far out of whack, there will be too few workers or too many retirees. That's what's happening. People are having fewer children. Birth rates in the U.S. are at the lowest levels since they started keeping records decades ago. This is a problem! Add to that the way that technology is going to change the workforce and we're in trouble. The forecast is that in ten to fifteen years, artificial intelligence is going to take over some industries completely.

And it's not just the U.S. grappling with this. Finland's fertility rate is below the U.S. rate. They base their healthcare system on the same faulty assumption that the population will continue to grow. Yet now there aren't enough young people to pay into the system to support the older people who use more healthcare. Most of Europe is even worse off. The combined E.U. fertility rate is just 1.59 babies over the course of a woman's lifetime, well below replacement levels. Japan is far more restrictive on immigration compared to the U.S. and the E.U. and is on the cutting edge of automation. Japan's fertility rate is just 1.4 and it has one of the oldest populations in the world. The one child policy that China had in place for decades is already putting a strain on the middle class. By 2050, 44% of the population is expected to be dependent elderly.

It's important to understand that monumental change is coming. There is a paradigm shift in the structure of retirement. You can't rely on the next generation for retirement income anymore.

This is a system that is collapsing under its own weight. And the craziest part is that the Social Security Administration forecasts that if nothing changes, the money will be gone in 2035. Social Security funds will be depleted within the next fifteen years if our government doesn't intervene! I'm talking about *your* retirement money. Why isn't our government doing something about this?

It's not looking good for your retirement benefits, is it? The good news is, you *can* avoid paying taxes on your Social Security. To be secure, you have to take matters into your own hands. If you're retired now or about to retire, you might be fine. You can probably ride it out before the entire system has to be reset. But if you're fifty or younger, Social Security will run out of money before you're able to start collecting. The younger you are, the surer you can be that these retirement systems won't be available to you. That also means you have to do something about it. Several countries have options for self-directed retirement accounts. In the U.S., a solo 401(k) is a great option for anyone with side or self-employment income.

If you are three, five, ten years away from retirement, do you want to pay taxes on retirement or not? Do you want to get double taxed on Social Security? There are ways to avoid it. And I'm not talking about locking your money away for fourteen years in a terrible low-paying annuity. There are other places to put your money besides annuities, CDs, mutual funds. The volatility of the market is terrible right now. No one can argue that. Any money you can save on taxes and funnel into your private retirement account will be compounded year to year instead of flushed down the toilet. In chapter 7 we'll talk about what you can do to avoid double taxation on Social Security.

Chapter 7

Avoiding Double Taxation on Social Security

Over and over again courts have said that there is nothing sinister in so arranging one's affairs as to keep taxes as low as possible. Everybody does so, rich or poor; and all do right, for nobody owes any public duty to pay more than the law demands: taxes are enforced exactions, not voluntary contributions. To demand more in the name of morals is mere cant.

—Judge Learned Hand

In America, there are two tax systems: one for the informed and one for the uninformed. Both are legal.

—Judge Learned Hand

I meet a lot of people who are surprised to hear they're going to be taxed once they start to receive their Social Security benefits. Realizing their benefits are subject to tax when their income surpasses the $25,000 for individual or $32,000 for married threshold feels unfair. The corrupt government in this Ponzi scheme calls this *provisional income*: your total income from wages, taxable and nontaxable interest, dividends, pensions, self-employment and other taxable income plus half of your annual Social Security benefits.[26] You work your butt off for 35–40 years and scrape together a million dollars in your 401(k), only to find out that when you draw that money, it's pushing you over the threshold and making your Social Security benefits taxable. It's a kick in the pants!

Social Security is not an entitlement program. That's your money. I believe the government is giving you the middle finger every paycheck, telling you, "We're better at managing your money than you are, so we're going to take it."

The government may call your retirement earnings "provisional income," but it's just a fancy way of naming the number beyond which you're going to be double taxed on your Social Security. It doesn't matter if you have rental property—it doesn't matter what the income is. If you're married and filing jointly and you have $44,000 or more of

---

26 "Social Security and Taxes," AARP, accessed October 9, 2015, https://www.aarp.org/content/dam/aarp/work/social_security/2011-10/Social-Security-and-Taxes.pdf

income, 85% of the amount of Social Security you received for that year is going to be double taxed for whatever rate you're in.

BUT there is a way you can avoid getting double taxed on Social Security. There's a well-kept secret I'd love to tell you about. This is an alternative strategy that very few people are using that relies on leveraging and financing and takes advantage of arbitrage. It is a Tier 1 asset, NOT an annuity. It's been around for over a hundred years and is very similar to a Roth IRA.

Here's the deal: best case scenario, Social Security is miraculously saved, and you have extra money for your retirement. Not a bad outcome! But if current political and economic conditions persist, a Social Security Hail Mary is unlikely, and we can't afford to put all our eggs in the government basket. But we can optimize the current U.S. tax code for our benefit.

There are ways to make contributions and to receive a deduction. There are ways to receive income in retirement (or whenever you want it) that are not reportable to the government. You don't even put it on the 1040. Yes, it's real.

Are you curious? You're not going to hear about this from your traditional financial guru. Those guys want to funnel everything through Wall Street—mutual funds, rip-off annuities—locking your money up in fees. This is a strategy I can't go into detail about here in the book. Reach out to me to find out if this amazing opportunity can work for you. Visit my website at sagemoneyradio.com, click Contact, and send me an email. I can't wait to tell you about this alternative strategy to help you avoid double taxation and keep your money in your pocket where it belongs.

Conclusion

Mount Everest, the highest summit in the world, stands at 30,000 feet. It attracts hundreds of climbers each year. Out of every 100 people that make it to the top, 7 die. Even more shocking is that 56% of all deaths occur *after* they made it to the summit. Those 7 may have made it up the mountain, but they didn't make it home. So did those 7 out of 100 succeed or fail? It really depends on their goal.

Financial planning can feel a lot like climbing Mount Everest. And your success or failure depends on your personal goals. So, what is your goal? Is it to accumulate the biggest number? Or is your goal to have a reliable long-term security net?

It has everything to do with what you're concentrating on. The bigger number, the better rate of return, or the benefit that can be achieved if you set your sights on your distributions. Have you ever had a conversation about the distribution side of your money and paying less in taxes?

On the way up the retirement mountain, are you minimizing your taxes as much as possible so you can accumulate more, or are you paying your fair share as you climb so when you descend you don't have a tax burden hanging around your neck?

Do you believe as I do that we should only be required to pay taxes once? Only on the money we earn and not on the money that our money earns. It makes a significant difference in your retirement years.

I would love to work with you and be your financial Mount Everest guide. I can show you what some of the ultra-wealthy are doing to lessen their tax burden. I've had the opportunity to interview some of those folks myself. I've listened to their regrets and discovered what they wish they'd known thirty years ago.

I hope I've convinced you that the conventional financial advice out there is not serving you and isn't in your best interest. If you're interested in putting more of your money in your own pocket instead of handing it over to Uncle Sam, I want to work with you. This isn't some shady, fringe strategy. I'm talking about optimizing the current U.S. tax code. I want to help you decrease your tax burden to the U.S. government. I can show you how to take deductions every single year. If you're ready to take your money back into your own hands, I want to work with you. Visit sagemoneyradio.com, click Contact, and send me a message.

Acknowledgments

I want to thank my two best friends, Brian Cohn and Sean Cangelosi. Brian and Sean, you are two amazing men, and I'm grateful to you, to your wives, and to your children for our many years of true friendship. Your support runs deep and has kept me afloat through many hard times. I have leaned on your advice, your rock-solid foundation, and your steadfast presence in more ways than I can count. Both of you define what a friend, husband, brother, and father should be. Your loyalty as a friend has been perpetual. I hope mine has been to both of you, as well. Every man needs two men like Brian and Sean in their life.

Thank you to Brennan Easley, another amazing friend of mine. Brennan, your business knowledge, savvy advice, and personal support have seen me through some tough decisions. I can't overstate how grateful I am for the wisdom you've shared with me over the years, and I'm grateful that we speak often. Your friendship, expertise, and insight have been invaluable through the years. Your approach to making a big decision that affects many people while keeping the emotions absent is admirable. It has been a joy to watch you and your wife raise your wonderful kids through the years. You are both terrific parents and people. You are the textbook definition of a businessman and family man.

I write this book in memory of my dad. He was the epitome of a great father, friend, and grandfather. Dad, I think of you every day. You were the embodiment of faithfulness. You never failed to get up and go to work, and I know now what you sacrificed to provide a better life for our family. I strive every day to live up to your example. I cherish the many hours we spent in the woods hunting and on the water fishing. I think about them every day. I love you and miss you dearly!

I'd like to thank my sister, Hollea, for always being there for me. Hollea, you are a strong and determined woman and a great sister.

I am incredibly grateful and blessed by my four kids. Patrick, Ruston, Katey, and Mollee—you are solid and respectable kids, and I know that with hard work and the grit you so obviously possess, you can accomplish anything you hope for in this life. I have enjoyed watching many hours of competition on the football, baseball, and softball fields and on basketball courts. Those wins and losses in competition are symbolic of the wins and losses in life. All four of you have taught me marvelous life lessons and have made a huge impact on me; because of you, I'm a better man. It is rare that four siblings enjoy each other's company as much as you do. It's an absolute pleasure to watch the four of you when you're together. My prayer is that you stay connected to each other and to our Heavenly Father throughout your life. I love all four of you so much!

I want to thank every single member of the United States Armed Forces. I am profoundly grateful to be an American citizen, and I see the many sacrifices these brave men and women have made and continue to make in service to this country. Every man and woman in our military is a true hero. I know my words don't do justice to how grateful I am for how willingly they sacrifice so much of their personal lives so our civilian lives can be what they are.

Finally, I want to thank Almighty God for creating me to walk on this earth. I truly know that every good and perfect gift comes from you.

Acknowledge and take to heart this day that the LORD is God in heaven above and on the earth below. There is no other.

Deuteronomy 4:39 (NIV)

About the Author

Hollis Day Jr. is the wise, witty voice of Sage Money Radio. Old fashioned and loyal to the core, Hollis believes he should have been born in the days of Mayberry when a man's word and a solid handshake were all you needed. He attributes this true-grit attitude to his father, who "sweated for a living" as the owner of a tire business.

Hollis graduated from Louisiana Tech University in 1999 with a business administration degree. Over the next 10 years he held multiple positions—high school football and baseball coach, nursing home administrator, and pharmaceutical sales representative.

Now Hollis specializes in alternative strategies and brings his passion to the people through AM 1150 WJBO radio in Baton Rouge, LA. His mission is to offer listeners and clients a commonsense approach to their financial future.

With an emphasis on protection from the volatility of Wall Street and developing a clear exit strategy, his firm provides niche financial coaching to individuals across the country.

To learn more or to request a consultation,
visit **SageMoneyRadio.com**.

About the Author

Help Me Pay It Forward

Thanks so much for purchasing and reading through this short book. It's a distillation of strategies I've learned, and what I wish I knew to protect my family's investment before tragedy struck. I hope you find this information useful and that it empowers you to make smarter investment decisions for your own financial future.

And on that note, would you please help me pay it forward? This information is only as helpful as its reach is wide. Readers look to reviews to make buying decisions, and honest feedback helps new readers find this.

Please take just a moment of your time to share your feedback on Amazon, Goodreads or wherever you found this title. It would mean the world to me, and would help in my mission to make each of us more resilient to a corrupt and untrustworthy system.

Thanks again for reading and
for any thoughts you share.

Made in United States
Orlando, FL
10 November 2026

90498877R10039